EMANCIPATION

"*Oneing*" is an old English word that was used by Lady Julian of Norwich (1342-1416) to describe the encounter between God and the soul. The Center for Action and Contemplation proudly borrows the word to express the divine unity that stands behind all of the divisions, dichotomies, and dualisms in the world. We pray and publish with Jesus' words, "that all may be one" (John 17:21).

EDITOR:
Vanessa Guerin

PUBLISHER:
The Center for Action and Contemplation

ADVISORY BOARD:
David Benner
James Danaher
Ilia Delio, OSF
Sheryl Fullerton
Marion Küstenmacher

Design and Composition by Nelson Kane Design

Woodcut illustrations by Kent Ambler

© 2015 The Center for Action and Contemplation.
All rights reserved.

Oneing
VOLUME 3 NO. 1

RICHARD ROHR, OFM
   Introduction   11

ERNESTO CARDENAL
   Psalm 5 (a paraphrase)   13

ILIA DELIO, OSF
   The Power of "Yes"   15

RABBI KENNETH CHELST
   Exodus through the Lens of Emancipation   21

CHRIS and PHILEENA HEUERTZ
   Emancipation and Identity:
      Reflections from a Red-Light District   29

SIMONE CAMPBELL, SSS
   The Shackles of Our Time   35

TIMOTHY P. SHRIVER
   Schooling the Heart   41

THE REV. PAUL FROMBERG
   Recipe Cards, Remembrance, and Emancipation   47

PAULA D'ARCY
   The Freedom of the Greater Heart   53

MIRABAI STARR
   Exquisite Risk:
      John of the Cross and the
      Transformational Power of Captivity   59

NOTES   65

EDITOR'S NOTE

Emancipation from the bondage of the soil is no freedom for the tree.
—Rabindranath Tagore

THIS QUOTE FROM Bengali Renaissance man and Nobel Prize recipient Rabindranath Tagore best expresses the underlying intent of much of the content in this edition of *Oneing*, transforming our understanding of the word "emancipation."

Typically we think of emancipation in terms of freedom or liberation from someone or something. In other words, freedom requires separation from whomever or whatever we believe holds us in bondage. However, Tagore's paradoxical words suggest that, even in bondage, emancipation is possible. An example would be the great Nelson Mandela. An influential man in his native South Africa, he became even more prominent during his twenty-seven years of incarceration. His spirit was not crushed by the damp, dark cell in which he spent most of his imprisonment; instead, it grew and expanded beyond the prison walls, transforming the lives of many, including his own.

Another prisoner transformed by his incarceration was the 16th-century Carmelite monk and mystic, St. John of the Cross. In her article, "Exquisite Risk," Mirabai Starr writes of the "Transformational Power of [his] Captivity." Imprisoned by his own Carmelite brothers, John spent nine months in a tiny cell. It was during this time of captivity and persecution that he experienced profound mystical union with the Divine and expressed his experiences in the form of timeless, ecstatic poetry. He later wrote commentaries to his major poems which, together with the poetry, have inspired not only Carmelite scholars but five centuries of Christians and other religious practitioners around the world.

There are many people who experience freedom in the midst of unrelenting trauma by discovering who they truly are in the "bondage of the soil" in which they grow. Chris and Phileena Heuertz, in their article, "Emancipation and Identity," compassionately part the curtains for a look at a notorious red-light district in Kolkata, India, where women and children alike are forced into prostitution. Through their eyes, we discover the means by which some of these women have been able to encounter their truest selves.

From liberation theologian Ernesto Cardenal's surprising paraphrase of Psalm 5, through Ilia Delio's article on "The Power of 'Yes,'" to Rabbi Kenneth Chelst's fresh exegesis of the Hebrew biblical texts, based on his study of the American slave experience, your understanding of emancipation will surely be expanded.

The tree's freedom isn't so obvious above the soil but, like the swallow that swoops around her leaves and rests within her branches, her roots are free to expand and grow through the moist soil of her grounding.

Vanessa Guerin,
Editor

CONTRIBUTORS

RICHARD ROHR, OFM, is a Franciscan of the New Mexico Province and the Founding Director of the Center for Action and Contemplation (CAC) in Albuquerque, New Mexico. An internationally-recognized author and spiritual leader, Fr. Richard teaches primarily on incarnational mysticism, non-dual consciousness, and contemplation, with a particular emphasis on how these affect the social justice issues of our time. Along with many recorded conferences, he is the author of numerous books, including the newly-released *Eager to Love: The Alternative Way of Francis of Assisi* and *Dancing Standing Still: Healing the World from a Place of Prayer*, an updated edition of *A Lever and a Place to Stand*. To learn more about Fr. Richard Rohr and the CAC, visit cac.org.

ILIA DELIO, OSF, a Franciscan Sister, lives in Washington, DC and is Director of Catholic Studies at Georgetown University, where she is also Visiting Professor. Prior to this position, Sr. Ilia was a Senior Research Fellow at Woodstock Theological Center, concentrating in the area of Science and Religion, and Professor and Chair of Spirituality Studies at Washington Theological Union, where she taught courses in the History of Christianity, Franciscan Theology, and Science and Religion. She holds a doctorate in Pharmacology from Rutgers University-New Jersey Medical School and a doctorate in Historical Theology from Fordham University. Ilia is the author of fourteen books, including *Christ in Evolution*, *The Emergent Christ*, *Simply Bonaventure*, *Care for Creation*—which won two Catholic Press Book Awards in 2009, *The Unbearable Wholeness of Being*, and *From Teilhard to Omega*. To learn more about Sr. Ilia Delio, visit explore.georgetown.edu/people/id72/.

RABBI KENNETH CHELST, PHD, is Professor of Operations Research and the Director of Engineering Management in the Department of Industrial and Systems Engineering at Wayne State University in Detroit, Michigan. He received a BA degree from Yeshiva University, an MS in operations research from New York University, and a PhD in operations research from MIT. He received rabbinic ordination from RIETS, an affiliate of Yeshiva University. He is author of *Exodus and Emancipation: Biblical and African-American Slavery*, and co-author of *Does This Line Ever Move?: Everyday Applications of Operations Research* and the textbook, *Value-Added Decision Making for Managers*. He was a recipient of the Edelman Prize Finalist Award for the best application of operations research in 2000. In 2011, the Institute for Operations Research and the Management Sciences awarded Dr. Chelst the prestigious President's Award for his contributions to society. To learn more about Kenneth Chelst, visit engineering.wayne.edu/profile/kenneth.chelst/.

CHRIS AND PHILEENA HEUERTZ have spent their lives bearing witness to hope—living, working, and traveling in over seventy countries, serving among the most vulnerable of the world's poor. Forerunners of the New Friar movement, Phileena and Chris have helped nurture and nourish communities around the world, focusing on anti-human trafficking initiatives for much of the past twenty years. In 2012, Phileena and Chris founded Gravity, a Center for Contemplative Activism, to support the development of consciousness by making contemplative practice accessible to individuals, communities, and organizations. Named Outstanding Alumni by Asbury University and Merging Influencers Reshaping Leadership by *Outreach* magazine, Phileena and Chris are both members of The Red Letter Christians Fellowship and speak all over the world at conferences, churches, college campuses, and retreats. Phileena is the author of *Pilgrimage of a Soul*; Chris' published books include *Simple Spirituality*, *Friendship at the Margins*, and *Unexpected Gifts*. To learn more about Chris and Phileena Heuertz and Gravity, visit gravitycenter.com.

SIMONE CAMPBELL, SSS, is a religious leader, attorney, and poet with extensive experience in public policy and advocacy for systemic change. She has been the Executive Director of NETWORK, a national Catholic social justice lobby, since 2004. Prior to that time, Sr. Simone served as Executive Director of JERICHO, a California interfaith public policy organization protecting the interests of people living in poverty. A noted speaker and educator on issues of justice, and the author of *A Nun on the Bus: How All of Us Can Create Hope, Change, and Community*, Sr. Simone has led three cross-country "Nuns on the Bus" trips, highlighting issues of economic justice, immigration reform, and civic participation. As the General Director of her religious community, the Sisters of Social Service, Sr. Simone has negotiated with both government and religious leaders. Her frequent national and international media appearances have included *60 Minutes*, *The Colbert Report*, and *The Daily Show with Jon Stewart*. To learn more about Sr. Simone Campbell and NETWORK, visit networklobby.org.

TIMOTHY P. SHRIVER, PHD, a social leader, educator, activist, film producer, and business entrepreneur, is the Chairman of Special Olympics and, in that capacity, serves 4.4 million Special Olympics athletes and their families in 170 countries. He has helped transform Special Olympics into a global movement that focuses on acceptance, inclusion, and respect for individuals with intellectual disabilities. As part of his passion for promoting the gifts of the forgotten, Tim has harnessed the power of film and television to share stories of inspiration and change through movies such as *Amistad* and *The Ringer*; shows on ABC, TNT, and NBC; and appearances on *The Today Show*, *Good Morning America*, and *Super Soul Sunday*. In 2011, Tim was recognized by *The Huffington Post* as one of the top 100 Game Changers. He has authored articles in many leading publications, including *The New York Times*, *The Washington Post*, *The Huffington Post*, and *Commonweal*, and is the author of *Fully Alive: Discovering What Matters Most*. To learn more about Timothy Shriver and the work of Special Olympics, visit specialolympics.org.

THE REV. PAUL FROMBERG, DMIN, is the rector of St. Gregory of Nyssa Episcopal Church in San Francisco. From 1987–2004, he served at Christ Church Cathedral and St. Andrew's Church, both in Houston. Paul is an iconographer and multimedia artist. He has taught courses in liturgics and congregational development at Virginia Theological Seminary and the Church Divinity School of the Pacific, where he received his doctor of ministry degree in 2014. He is also a consultant with congregations across the country. He is an active participant in emergent church conversation groups and has been a speaker at the Wild Goose Festival and the Greenbelt Festival in Great Britain. To learn more about Paul Fromberg and St. Gregory of Nyssa Episcopal Church, visit saintgregorys.org.

PAULA D'ARCY, a former psychotherapist, leads retreats and seminars worldwide and is a frequent teacher in the sabbatical program at Oblate School of Theology in San Antonio, Texas. The work of Red Bird Foundation, Paula's non-profit organization, includes prison retreats and talks, and the creation of small groups of individuals—including Israeli and Palestinian men and women—to foster widening awareness of the world's ongoing work toward freedom and peace. The author of numerous books, including *Gift of the Red Bird* and *Waking Up to This Day*, Paula's journey began in 1975 with the sudden death of her husband and daughter in a drunk-driving accident. Paula and her surviving daughter now make their home in Texas. To learn more about Paula D'Arcy and her foundation, visit redbirdfoundation.com.

MIRABAI STARR writes creative non-fiction and translates sacred literature. She is Professor of Philosophy and World Religions at University of New Mexico–Taos speaks internationally on contemplative practice and interspiritual dialogue. A certified bereavement counselor, Mirabai helps mourners harness the transformational power of loss. She has received critical acclaim for her revolutionary translations of *Dark Night of the Soul* by St. John of the Cross, *The Interior Castle* and *The Book of My Life* by St. Teresa of Avila, and *The Showings* of Julian of Norwich. She is author of the 6-volume Sounds True series *Contemplations, Prayers, and Living Wisdom*. Her poetry collection, *Mother of God Similar to Fire*, is a collaboration with iconographer William Hart McNichols. *God of Love: A Guide to the Heart of Judaism, Christianity and Islam*—winner of the New Mexico/Arizona Book Award for Religion and the Nautilus Gold Award in Western Spirituality, and named one of the Best Spiritual Books of 2012 by *Spirituality & Practice*—positions Mirabai at the forefront of the emerging Interspiritual Movement. To learn more about Mirabai Starr, visit mirabaistarr.com.

INTRODUCTION

Perhaps you may wonder why we chose the precise word "emancipation" as our theme for this edition of *Oneing*, instead of the more common word "freedom." I take the risk of using emancipation in a specific way, to encourage us to think anew.

I will begin by giving you a dictionary definition of emancipation: "To be set free from legal, social, or political restrictions." Emancipation directs our attention to a systemic level of freedom rather than just the personal freedoms enjoyed by individuals. To move our attention to this deeper and broader level, I am using the term emancipation to refer to the larger freedom few of us enjoy, which is actually quite scary. With the exception of those who are fully emancipated, we each live inside our own smaller security systems, political correctnesses, cultures, and eras—quiet, even secret, agreements that are "too big to fail."

Americans, for example, rightly revel in the fact that we enjoy certain rights and freedoms from restraints (free markets, free speech, the freedom to be secure and to defend ourselves). We typically pay little attention to the fact that these liberties ultimately depend on an interior freedom within oneself, and a total dependence on the system itself—which, paradoxically, can never fully guarantee or deliver these very freedoms. Our inability to recognize this has made our so-called freedoms very selective, class-based, often dishonest, and open to bias.

For example, are we free to think or imagine that there could be alternatives to our free-market system? Largely, we are likely to be called dangerous or un-American if we dare broach the topic. We believe in free speech, but know better than to claim that money is actually what controls our elections, rather than "one person, one vote." How many of us feel free to publicly praise an island country like Cuba? Does our freedom to protect ourselves (gun rights, limitless military spending) give us the right and freedom to use the vast majority of the natural and economic resources of our country for our protection? Even if it means not providing food, healthcare, or education for the same people that we say we are securing? Do we even have the freedom to politely ask that question during the course of ordinary cocktail-party conversation? I think you begin to see how rare full emancipation may be; how we mostly talk only about the freedoms which exist within agreed-upon boxes.

Only citizenship in a much larger "Kingdom of God" is the antidote to confinement within those well-hidden, yet agreed-upon, boxes. In fact, because they are foundational and necessary cultural agreements, we do not even recognize them as boxes. When we place all of our identity in our one country, class, or ethnic group, we are unable to imagine another way of thinking.

To be fair, sometimes such boxes are good, helpful, and even necessary! These silent agreements allow cultures to function and people to work together. But my job, and the job of any spiritual wisdom, is to tell you that "We are fellow citizens with the saints and part of God's household" (Eph 2:19), and thus "Our citizenship is in heaven" (Phil 3:20). We have been called to live in the biggest box of all, while still working and thinking inside of smaller boxes. That is a necessarily creative and difficult tension, yet it is really the only way we can enjoy all levels of freedom.

So we will use the word emancipation to describe a deeper, bigger, and scarier level of freedom: inner, outer, personal, economic, structural, and spiritual—all at once. Surely this is the task of a lifetime. Those who achieve this level of emancipation really are "from another world" and, frankly, disturb and irritate those invested in smaller security systems. Precisely because they cannot be bribed by payoffs, punishments, and rewards, their insider/outsider status allows them to be fully and freely involved in this world. Their final and full freedom is that *they do not need to buck the system or see themselves as outsiders or mavericks at all.* They simply are.

Richard Rohr, OFM

Psalm 5 *(a paraphrase)*

Give ear to my words, O Lord
Hearken unto my moaning
Pay heed to my protest
For you are not a God friendly to dictators
neither are you a partisan of their politics
Nor are you influenced by their propaganda
Neither are you in league with the gangster

There is no sincerity in their speeches
nor in their press releases

They speak of peace in their speeches
while they increase their war production
They speak of peace at Peace Conferences
and secretly prepare for war
Their lying radios roar into the night
Their desks are strewn with criminal intentions and sinister reports
But you will deliver me from their plans
They speak through the mouth of the submachine gun
Their flashing tongues are bayonets....

Punish them, O Lord,
thwart them in their policies
confuse their memorandums
obstruct their programs

At the hour of Alarm
you shall be with me
you shall be my refuge on the day of the Bomb
To him who believes not in the lies of their commercial messages
nor in their publicity campaigns nor in their political campaigns
you will give your blessing
With love do you encompass him
As with armor-plated tanks.

—by Ernesto Cardenal, translated by Robert Marquez[1]

The Power of "Yes"

By Ilia Delio, OSF

IN MAY 2014, I celebrated my Silver Jubilee as a Franciscan Sister. Twenty-five years ago (actually thirty years ago, since I began religious life as a Discalced Carmelite nun), I said "yes" to a single-hearted relationship with God. I can say, *prima facie*, I did not know what I was getting into when I said "yes" (probably just as well!), but I do know the word arose out of a much deeper center than my well-oiled, academic brain. The good news is that my "yes" has grown much deeper and wider than I could have ever imagined. I want to use this opportunity to reflect on the power of "yes" and the implications of this word for evolving life today.

I suppose I should begin an essay on the word "yes" with human language, but in reality there is a great "yes" resounding throughout the long span of cosmic evolution. The epic of evolution may be the greatest story ever told, because it speaks of the world's struggle to move toward an expansive freedom in the presence of self-giving grace. Nature is dynamic and integrative, oriented toward increasing levels of complex life. Evolution helps us realize that God works through the openness of creation and is less concerned with imposing design on processes than with providing nature with opportunities to participate in its own creation. Evolution reflects nature's faithful "yes" to new life and to the creativity of future.

The story of humans within evolutionary history begins around 4.5 billion years ago, when the earth and other planets began forming around the young sun. Over this long period of time, life evolved from enucleated bacterial cells to nucleated cells, which would eventually replicate into multicellular animals. Humans, as mammals, have existed on earth for a relatively short time—only about 0.04% of that 4.5 billion years. The modern human physique first appeared in Africa about 150,000 years ago, then spread into the rest of the Old World, replacing existing populations of archaic human forms.[1] Diarmuid O'Murchu indicates that humans and our most immediate hominid ancestors evolved as hunters and gatherers in small tribes and extended families.

The entire history of the universe, and particularly the history of biological life on the earth, has been characterized by the steady emergence of complexity. The term emergence is used today to describe the appearance of novelty in nature. Emergence is irreducible novelty of increasing complexity, a combination of holism with novelty in a way that contrasts with both physical reductionism and dualism. Philip Clayton defines emergence as "genuinely new properties which are not reducible to what came before, although they are continuous with it." He writes further: "Once there was no universe and then, after the Big Bang, there was an exploding world of stars and galaxies. Once the earth was unpopulated and later it was teeming with primitive life forms."[2] From galaxies to Gandhi, emergence may be a way the Big Bang repeats itself as the universe continues to unfold.

The human person is integrally part of evolution in that we rise from the process; however, in reflecting on the process, we stand apart from it. Teilhard de Chardin said that the human person "is nothing else than evolution become conscious of itself." To this idea he added, "The consciousness of each of us is evolution looking at itself and reflecting upon itself."[3] Thus the human person emerges from evolution. She/he is "the point of emergence in nature, at which this deep cosmic evolution culminates and declares itself."[4] We are evolution made conscious of itself.

Cosmogenesis and evolution can be described as a great cosmic "yes." Every star, quark, atom, and cell radiate a fullness of life with

We are evolution made conscious of itself.

their "yes" to life. Up to the emergence of the human person, truth and existence are unified. A tree does nothing more than be a tree, Thomas Merton suggested, and, in being a tree, it gives glory to God.[5] The truth of the tree is its "treeness"; it can do nothing other than be a tree and, in being what it is created to be, it radiates divine love and wisdom. The human person, however, utters the first "no" in cosmic history, a conscious rejection of cosmic community and evolving life. The mark of the human species is symbolic language. We have the capacity to use words that express a complexity of ideas. This capacity is unique (as far as we know) in cosmic life. The human person emerges with the capacity to reflect, to act freely, and to say "no." The human "no" is the rejection of communion and thus of nature's intrinsic need for wholeness. The human "no" is symbolized by the story of Adam and Eve (Gn 3:1-17). We might describe this "no" ("I will not obey") as cosmic sin, the Adamic disconnect and disruption of evolution.

The human, therefore, is the first to consciously reject divine Love and thus reject participation in the ongoing evolution of life. The human "no" is the act of symbolic self-assertion and independence that disrupts nature's cosmic communion. The 5th-century theologian Maximus the Confessor said that Adam's "no" was the peak of human freedom.[6] Adam thought that only a person who can say "no" is truly free; that if one is to achieve one's freedom, the human must be able to say "no" to God. Adam's "no" was the first real "no" to integral wholeness in the history of the universe; the conscious "no," uttered as an act of freedom over and against God; the "no" that splintered the undivided whole of cosmotheandric love into a thousand little pieces.

This is why Mary's "yes" is like a new singularity, an explosion of new life through the boundless surrender to divine love: *fiat voluntas tua*. Her "yes" speaks to us of being grasped by divine Love, trusting that she belonged to another, to a whole, to God and all that is of God. Mary returns nature to nature. Her "yes" speaks of surrender and the realization that life is no life unless it is given over to Life

We are called to realize our participation in the unfolding of cosmic life, as creation seeks its ultimate fulfillment in God.

itself. Jesus' own suffering and death expressed his life as one lived for others. His mission of creative whole-making returns humanity to its integral nature within the whole of evolutionary nature and reveals the way of human evolution toward wholeness and peace. Through the life of Jesus we see ourselves as part of an ongoing process of creative and emergent life. This wholeness of life is the Christ, who is seeking to come to birth within us—like Mary—by our "yes" to the flow of divine Love. We are called to realize our participation in the unfolding of cosmic life, as creation seeks its ultimate fulfillment in God.

We are losing the power of "yes" today. Nature is in turmoil: broken, abandoned, and abused. Evolution is stifled and the world seems to be spinning out of control. The internet has turned "yes" into autonomy and managed grace. I can say "yes" online while saying "no" in my heart—"no," I really *don't* want to be friends with this person; "no," I don't want any demands other than this connection. This type of ambivalence or duplicity has filtered into every aspect of our lives, including politics, business, and social relations, where "yes" means "this is good for me" and "no" means "not for me." It is the duplicity of failed marriages and relationships, including those of religious life. I can say "yes" at the altar or at the feet of a bishop, but in my heart I don't want to be part of anything or anyone; I want to be alone. I can say "yes" to the vows of poverty and obedience and live a hidden, spendthrift life of luxury. I can say "yes" and mean "no" when reality and virtual reality appear seamless and I can no longer discern the virtual from the real.

The word "yes" is an I–Thou relatedness; it does not begin with myself, but with the other who completes myself because I recognize something of myself in the other. The 9th-century Muslim poet Mansur al-Hallaj expressed this oneness beautifully when he wrote:

> I am the One whom I love
> And the One whom I love is I—
> Two breaths and spirits sharing one body.
> And when you see the One, you see us both.[7]

By saying "no" to another, we reject our relationship with another; we reject being part of a whole and participating in evolving life. By saying "no," we thwart cosmic evolution; we unravel cosmic history. I do not mean here a moral "no" but an existential "no" that renders us unnatural and consigned to an exile of unrelatedness. That is why Mary's "yes" symbolizes cosmotheandric evolution; the whole cosmos is, in a sense, *Theotokos*, God-bearing life. God desires to share life with us, to be with us, and co-create with us a new future of life together. To say "yes" to this God of unquenchable love is to be conscious of belonging to another; to realize that the I of my "I" is the Thou of my heart. We have always been one and, if I do not block the space of "yes" in my heart, then we shall become one, ever more deeply, forever. •

Exodus through the Lens of Emancipation

By Kenneth Chelst

More than thirty years ago, I began teaching adult education Bible classes. My goal was to enrich my understanding of the Hebrew Bible through in-depth study of the classical Jewish sources that I used to prepare for each class. Comprehension and insight were refined by the give-and-take that enlivened each session. To keep participants engaged, I strove to provide novel perspectives and concretize key concepts while staying within traditional Jewish interpretations of the narrative.

I had little idea at the time how African-American slave history would become a touchstone that helped me frame and interpret numerous texts, and uncover concepts that often lay just below the linguistic surface. I had no training in history and had never studied the African-American experience. In this essay, I will illustrate how this new frame of reference opened up new vistas of understanding and challenged me to explore issues I otherwise would have glossed over.

IDENTITY

MY NEW PERSPECTIVE can be demonstrated with the opening verse of the book of Exodus: "Now these are the names of the sons of Israel, who came into Egypt with Jacob; every man came with his household" (Ex 1:1).

It is a verse I had read hundreds of times, and it had never warranted a second thought. Now this verse reflects my understanding of the Israelite slave experience. It states that the Israelites had Hebrew names and came into Egypt as family units. The Midrash builds on this and related texts, making the point that there are three reasons the Israelites were worthy of redemption: They kept their Hebrew names,[1] their Hebrew language, and their family structure and sanctity.[2] This contrasts with the African-American experience: Masters quickly assigned slaves new names, the original language did not survive beyond the first generation, and the family unit was under constant attack.

Rabbi Soloveitchik, my teacher, commented on the verse: "Then thou shalt say unto thy son: 'We were Pharaoh's slaves in Egypt; and the LORD brought us out of Egypt with a mighty hand'" (Dt 6:21). This phrase, "We were Pharaoh's slaves in Egypt," forms the opening discussion of the Exodus narrative at the Passover Seder. Rabbi Soloveitchik argued that this political enslavement to Pharaoh produced an oppressive, faceless environment with no chance to flee or hope for a better master. In contrast with my teacher, I perceived a relative advantage of the Israelite's political enslavement to chattel slavery. The Israelites were able to keep and nourish a distinct cultural identity as they grew from a family into a people and, ultimately, a nation. This simple distinction between political slavery and chattel slavery led to insights spread over more than one hundred pages of analysis in my book *Exodus and Emancipation: Biblical and African-American Slavery*.

MEASURE FOR MEASURE

I used another frame of reference, the psychological needs of the oppressed victim, to explore parallels between the two slave experiences. The victim of a crime or long-term oppression has a need to see the oppressor punished for his or her crimes—ideally, measure for measure. God promised to Abram that when he freed his descendants from their enslavement, the oppressing nation would be punished and the Israelites would be compensated.

> And He said unto Abram: "Know of a surety that thy seed shall be a stranger in a land that is not theirs, and shall serve them; and they shall afflict them four hundred years; and also that nation, whom they shall serve, will I judge; and afterward shall they come out with great substance" (Gn 15:13-14).

A central element of the Exodus narrative is how plague after plague attacked the Egyptians as God's judgment, measure for measure. The first plague turned the Nile waters into blood and killed the fish. This told Pharaoh and his people that God had seen the drowning of Israelite sons. The book of judgment for this deed closed with the drowning of the Egyptian military in the Sea of Reeds. Egyptian magicians told Pharaoh, "This is the finger of God" (Ex 8:19). As the Egyptians lay dying on the shores of the Sea, the Bible records, "Israel saw the Great Hand that God used against the Egyptians" (Ex 14:31).

In the American Civil War, both sides were deeply religious and sought to sway God through prayer and national fast days. Abraham Lincoln considered the war's carnage punishment of both North and South for having allowed slavery to continue. In his second inaugural address, on March 4, 1865, he accepted the Civil War as God's justice, measure for measure.

> Yet, if God wills that it continue until all the wealth piled by the bondsman's two hundred and fifty years of unrequited toil shall be sunk, and until every drop of blood drawn with the lash shall be paid by another drawn with the sword, as was said three thousand years ago, so still it must be said, "the judgments of the Lord are true and righteous altogether" (Ps 19:9).

On the individual level, after hearing of the death of her mistress' last surviving child, one slave mother declared, "You sold all my children; God took yours. Not one to bury either of us. Now I forgive you."[3]

SELF-IMAGE

VICTIMIZATION CAN ALSO UNDERMINE a people's self-image, especially if it extends over many generations. Repairing this self-image cannot be a gift of God; It requires the active participation of victims to demonstrate their rebirth. For the Israelites, the public mass sacrifice of the paschal lamb, a god of Egypt, and its subsequent open-pit roasting, was an act of mass disobedience and a heroic action that demonstrated their trust in God. This was preceded by the individual commitment to reinstitute the practice of circumcision.

The African-American sacrifice took place once the Emancipation Proclamation gave blacks the authorization to join the Union Army. 180,000 served in the army and more than 38,000 were killed. Stories of their heroism in the northern press helped transform northern attitudes: "It is no longer possible to doubt the bravery and steadiness of the colored race."[4] Their newfound ability to serve in the army clearly impacted each individual's self-image. An African-American soldier declared, "Now we soldiers are men, men for the first time in our lives."[5]

My first exposure to American slave history was Frederick Douglass' powerful autobiography. This led me on a journey that has added depth to my understanding of the oppressiveness of all forms of slavery. At one stage during his slavery, Douglass was turned over to a slave breaker named Mr. Covey. Douglass writes:

> If at any one time of my life than another, I was made to drink the bitterest dregs of slavery, that time was during the first six months of my stay with Mr. Covey. We were worked in all weathers. It was never too hot nor too cold; it could never rain, blow, hail, or snow too hard, for us to work in the field. Work, work, work, was scarcely more than the order of the day than of the night. The longest days were too short for him, and the shortest nights, too long for him.[6]

How well this description parallels the Biblical narrative: "And they made their lives bitter with hard service, in mortar and in brick, and in all manner of service in the field; in all their service, wherein they made them serve with rigor" (Ex 1:14). When I read of Moses interfering with the beating of an Israelite, I imagined all the other beatings that were not interrupted, which broke the slave's spirit, as happened to Frederick Douglass.

> Mr. Covey succeeded in breaking me. I was broken in body, soul, and spirit. My natural elasticity was crushed, my intellect languished, the disposition to read departed, the cheerful spark that lingered about my eye died; the dark night of slavery closed in upon me; and behold a man transformed into a brute.[7]

Harriet A. Jacobs' autobiography, *Incidents in the Life of a Slave Girl*, provided a woman's perspective on the slave experience. She recalled her dilemma and ambivalence when her child was deathly ill:

> I loved to watch his infant slumbers; but always there was a dark cloud over my enjoyment. I could never forget that he was a slave. Sometimes I wished that he might die in infancy. God tried me. My darling became very ill. The bright eyes grew dull, and the little feet and hands were so icy cold that I thought death had already touched them. I had prayed for his death, but never so earnestly as I now prayed for his life; and my prayer was heard. Alas, what mockery it is for a slave mother to try to pray back her dying child to life! Death is better than slavery.[8]

I am the Lord, and I will bring you out from under the burdens of the Egyptians, and I will deliver you from their bondage.

—Ex 6:6-7

Harriet Jacobs' ambivalence about slave motherhood made me wonder what Moses' mother was thinking when she made her fateful decision.

> And the woman conceived, and bore a son; and when she saw that he was a goodly child, she hid him three months And when she could no longer hide him, she took for him an ark of bulrushes, and daubed it with slime and with pitch; and she put the child therein, and laid it in the flags by the river's brink (Ex 2:2-3).

EMANCIPATION

My search for understanding went both ways. The most notable phrase in the Exodus was God's demand, "Let my people go" (Ex 9:1). This, however, is an incomplete representation of the text. God actually demanded, "Let my people go, so that they may serve me." Freedom for the Israelite nation was not an end in itself. It was a first step toward the ultimate redemption that would occur at Mount Sinai with the giving of the Decalogue and, subsequently, the entire Pentateuch. Moses was charged to explain to the Israelites that they were to become God's people.

> Wherefore say unto the children of Israel: I am the Lord, and I will bring you out from under the burdens of the Egyptians, and I will deliver you from their bondage, and I will redeem you with an outstretched arm, and with great judgments; and I will take you to me for a people, and I will be to you a God; and ye shall know that I am the Lord your God, who brought you out from under the burdens of the Egyptians (Ex 6:6-7).

This led me to explore the hopes, dreams, and actions of former slaves as they became emancipated. In addition to economic and personal freedom, they yearned for what had been forbidden them as slaves: education and family. Slave owners feared the power of literacy, especially since the major slave rebellions were led by educated blacks. As a result, most states outlawed teaching slaves to read and write.[9] "I [Booker T. Washington] resolved that I should never be satisfied until I learned what the dangerous practice was like."[10] Former slaves recognized that education was necessary for economic survival. They also yearned "to read the word of the Lord." Slaves had serious doubts about the way masters and white preachers quoted the Bible to support the institution of slavery and demand obedience. Their passion led to revised state constitutions in the Deep South that, for the first time, included funding for public education.

Southern states did not offer legal status to slave marriages or protection for the family unit. However, slaves' desire for confirmation of marital status led to thousands upon thousands of marriages soon after emancipation, often in mass ceremonies. One army chaplain married 119 couples in a single hour.[11] In addition, after the war, legions of blacks traveled across the South to reunite with their families. All newspapers carried advertisements seeking lost relatives, the same way Holocaust survivors searched for family members after World War II.

SUMMARY

In the Introduction to this special issue entitled "Emancipation," Richard Rohr suggests the importance of stepping outside of our personal boxes, be they economic, structural, or spiritual. In part, the frames we use to structure our lives come from the country in which we live, the class to which we belong, or the ethnic group in which we take pride. In this essay, I have attempted to illustrate another form of emancipation: intellectual emancipation. I was educated in the orthodox Jewish tradition and have studied the Bible within this framework of a faith community and ethnic group. Fortunately, I was given the opportunity and the inspiration to see the Book of Exodus in a totally different historical and ethnic context. African-American slaves took comfort in the Israelite story of bondage and freedom, and prayed that God would similarly respond to their cries. As a result of my research, not only was I able to better understand how others might be inspired by the text, I also gained new insight into how God plays a role in the history of peoples and nations. In the adult classes I taught, I also challenged and engaged my students as they struggled with the creative tension engendered by this unusual approach to the Biblical narrative. •

Emancipation and Identity:
Reflections from a Red-Light District

By Chris and Phileena Heuertz

In Kolkata, India, one of the most notorious neighborhoods is just two blocks long, yet as many as ten to twelve thousand women and children are forced to prostitute up and down the tangle of its narrow, twisted alleyways. Many of those victimized in this red-light area were trafficked from rural parts of North India, Nepal, Bangladesh, and Burma. Torn away from any semblance of a support system and unable to speak the local language, many of these vulnerable women and children are trapped in a commercialized industry that profits off the sexual exploitation of human bodies.

Over the past fifteen years, we've become friends with a number of these women—some of them so poor they feel prostitution is their only option. Born into a hopeless cycle of poverty, a good number of the girls simply followed in the dire footsteps of their mothers and grandmothers who, in years past, were forced to sell their own bodies. Little girls were born into, and then grew up in, brothels where they quietly sat outside the door while their mothers "serviced" ten to fifteen men a day.

FREEDOM

Part of our work has included helping a small tactical community of idealists press into the pain of this neighborhood. As a community, we've quietly and slowly built a viable employment alternative. Hidden away in the same red-light area, a small-business initiative now offers hope and secures freedom. This inspiring microenterprise offers occupations with dignity for women exploited by the commercial sex industry.

Through this work of hope and peace, women of all ages are trained to make beautiful quilted blankets, scarves, and purses, and are then offered jobs in the company as a way out of prostitution. Made from recycled old saris, the products they sell are symbols of restoration. An apparently used up, discarded, and valueless object is artfully transformed into something beautiful—and, even more, something valuable.

These handicrafts dramatically symbolize freedom. The process of creating such goods is a prophetic image of what the company is doing within the sex trade—allowing women who have been enslaved to grow into greater freedom, and ultimately recover their true identities.

RECLAIMING THEIR NAMES

A common psychological coping mechanism of those who experience prolonged sexual abuse and trauma is to create false identities, or alter aliases, behind which they hide. Most of our friends who are forced to sell sex usually use false names when they are working, names such as "Pinky"— clearly not the names they were given by their families. As a form of self-preservation, they externalize those aliases so that abuse and exploitation are visited upon their alter personalities rather than their true selves. In the early stages of this small business initiative in Kolkata, the project director gathered all the women together to admire the beauty of their work. She held up some of the blankets and drew attention to each as an exquisite piece of art. A trained artist herself, she explained that artists sign their names to their work. The director then asked the women if they'd like to begin sewing signature tags into each of the blankets they made. The women agreed. When asked what name they'd like to use, in a surprising eruption of grace, most of the woman chose their real names: names that had been hidden (in some cases, for ten to fifteen years) the precious names given to the women when they were babies.

Reclaiming their names was a significant component of the slow and patient work of freedom, on a journey toward true identity.

A few years ago, one of our friends, a Grammy Award-winning singer-songwriter, included this business initiative from Kolkata in his "One Million Can" campaign. Our friend, together with the other musicians on his label, identified eight organizations they thought were doing important justice-related work in the world. While on tour, these musicians invited one million college students to give at least one dollar each to support this work.

One of the stops on our friend's tour was Omaha, so we took him out for lunch. As we sat at the table, we gave him a sari blanket as a gift of gratitude for the advocacy work he had done on behalf of the women in Kolkata. Later that night, during his concert, our friend brought the blanket onto the stage. The energy was great: a sold-out arena, an electrifying light show, huge video screens, and amazing music. Toward the end of the night, our friend dialed things down and set aside his guitar. He stood alone, center-stage, with a single spotlight shining on him. Behind a microphone, he gently held up his new sari blanket and began telling thousands of curious listeners the story of the women, our friends, in Kolkata. He shared about the aliases the women took on as a means of coping with the horrific abuse they experienced every day. As he reflected on how the women each had chosen her given name to put on her work, he searched for the signature tag on his blanket. Upon discovering it, he said, "And this one, this blanket, was made by a woman named Mukti."

Hearing Mukti's true name, spoken in an arena among thousands, was enough to make a grown man weep.

For much of her life, Mukti was held captive in the small prison of her brothel room. Forced to have sex with as many as a hundred customers per week, she was called awful, unspeakable things and learned at a young age to hide and protect her true identity. But that night, somewhere in mid-America, her name, her true identity, was safely brought out from hiding and celebrated.

It turns out that *mukti* is a derivative of the Indian philosophical and religious notion of *moksha*, which is literally translated as "emancipation" or "liberation." Simply put, mukti means "freedom." Mukti, a woman named Freedom. The name for which all of us are searching.

A woman, set free from a dehumanizing trade, claims her true identity by printing her given name on the quilt she has crafted. And, as her name reverberates in a stadium filled with thousands of people, we are reminded that this too is our task—to move from bondage to freedom, from enslavement to emancipation. To boldly come out from hiding and offer our truest selves to the world. This is the work of the spiritual journey. And, just like the making of beautiful quilts from discarded saris, it's slow and patient work.

A DARK SIDE

FREEDOM IS BEAUTIFUL but, as all things do, it has a dark side. Though hard to believe, some of the women we've worked with have returned to prostitution. This is often the case with those who have been institutionalized, incarcerated, or systematically held in bondage for long periods of time. Their captivity becomes an experience of security.

You and I are not so different. Life has a way of creating mental and emotional prisons; prisons constructed from fear. We fear we won't be accepted as we are, or we'll be hurt if we show up, so we hide and hold back, or pretend we're someone we're not. Oftentimes our egoic prison feels safer than the uncharted path of emancipation. Emancipation is the process of becoming who we truly are in God.

To the degree I am free, the world will be free. "The entire created world is groaning, as in the pains of childbirth, for this freedom" (Rom 8:22). It isn't a solitary journey; we are in it together. Our individual emancipation has a direct impact on the ability of all life-beings to grow and thrive with integrity.

But it is slow and patient work, and often we are not open to this mysterious, transformative labor of grace.

To boldly come out from hiding and offer our truest selves to the world. This is the work of the spiritual journey.

SOLITUDE

WE ARE SURROUNDED by people all the time—if not literally, at least virtually, through e-mails, texts, phone calls, Twitter feeds, Instagram notifications, and Facebook updates. Modern technology makes it all too easy to fill up space with lots of people and interactions. Ironically, while we're surrounded by others, many of us are still very lonely. Crowding our lives doesn't ease the loneliness. Only practices of solitude can do that.

But we don't know how to be alone, and we don't like to be alone. Many of us don't like to be alone because we don't know who we are. It often seems safer to avoid drawing near to our authentic selves than to take steps down the path of the unknown. Solitude gives us courage to take those first steps and become acquainted with the prisons that confine us. Over time, solitude teaches us how to be present—present to ourselves and to God, so that we can be truly present to others.

SILENCE

OUR LIVES ARE crowded and noisy. We've grown so used to the noise of technology, and the noise in our heads, that silence can be frightening. Noisy, full lives that allow no room for silence distract us from being able to hear and listen to the One who desires to be heard, known, and shared with the world. Silence helps us learn to listen to the voice of God in our lives, a voice that we've long tuned out and may not recognize. Silence allows us to listen to ourselves and to God, so that we can truly listen to others. As we listen, we grow more acquainted with our true and real names.

STILLNESS

A LOT OF US are working very hard to build a better world, all the while harming ourselves and others with our frenetic, well-meaning actions. Even in our best efforts to be involved in meaningful works of social justice, if our false selves are at work, there could be unintended and harmful consequences. The false self operates from a place of fear and control, infecting our attempts at good work with deceptive, self-serving interests. The spiritual journey is a process of being emancipated from such a prison. Stillness arrests our frenetic compulsions to reinforce the false self; compulsions that fuel misguided, selfish, and ego-driven motivations. As the false self diminishes, the true self is set free—free to engage in selfless acts of love, peace, and justice for the healing of our world.

Contemplative practice—practice marked by solitude, silence, and stillness—facilitates a very gentle emancipation from the false self into the True Self. Like Mukti, contemplation helps us reclaim the name most of us have forgotten: Freedom. This is the surprising gift of the spiritual journey: as time unfolds, our emancipation allows us to cooperate in the "birthing of a new world" (Rv 21:1). •

The Shackles of Our Time

By Simone Campbell, SSS

THE CONCEPT OF EMANCIPATION for me is rooted in the civil rights struggle of our nation. It was this struggle that fueled my youthful commitment and led to a lifetime of engagement. Dr. Martin Luther King, Jr., spoke eloquently, in his speeches and throughout his life, about the intersection of faith and justice. There is no division between the two; faith requires us to act for justice. As Pope Francis said in his homily on February 28, 2014, in the Church of Gesu, Rome, "An authentic faith always implies a deep desire to change the world." This is a journey out of bondage into freedom. In short, it is a journey of emancipation, much like the Exodus in the Hebrew Scriptures.

The shackles of our time, with which we are called to engage, are principally the economic disparities in our nation and around the world. The statistics are staggering; in the developed world, the United States has the greatest income and wealth disparities and the lowest social mobility. The "recovery" from the recent great recession has gone entirely to the top 10% of income-earners in our nation. The average CEO salary of a publicly traded company is $10 million a year (plus other benefits), while the workers, whose labor makes this wealth possible, are experiencing no increase in wages. In fact, since the 1980s, worker productivity has consistently risen while wages have basically stayed flat.

Millions of adult workers labor full-time for minimum wage ($15,000/year) and live in poverty. I met Robin, who works full-time for a profitable national clothing retailer, making slightly above minimum wage. She said to me, "You would never know by looking at me that I have to live in a homeless shelter because I can't afford rent in the DC area on my salary." This is the story of many workers in our nation. While grateful to have a job at all, they are shackled by low wages.

I have puzzled over the forces that create this situation. Do CEOs not know the consequences of their decisions not to raise wages? I had a chance to host a business roundtable to explore the intersection of business and the common good. Toward the end of our hour together, I asked the six entrepreneurs why CEOs making an average of $10 million per year were going for $11 million. My question was, "Are they not getting by on the $10 million?" To my surprise, one man quickly responded by saying, "Oh no, Sr. Simone! It isn't about the money! CEOs are very competitive and they want to win. Money is just the measure of winning." My response to this was a rather stunned, "Can't we change the measure to something a little less toxic?" The prize of money in the competitive world is shackling our nation and our people—but many are blind to their participation in creating this bondage.

Often I find that those who are not shackled by poverty want to define people living in poverty as lazy and "poor" decision-makers. When I get to hear the stories of the actual people who are struggling at the bottom of our economy, the situation is very different. Living in poverty is hard work.

I met Ann in rural New York. She told me that both she and her husband have master's degrees, but in the recession they both lost their jobs, lost their house, and moved with their four teenagers into a two-bedroom apartment. He is working seasonally in construction and she is working in a bookstore. Both are grateful for their jobs, but she stressed how much work it is to be poor. They don't have money

Emancipation happens when our contemplative journey takes us beyond ourselves into care for all and fighting for a vision that benefits the 100%.

to run the clothes dryer, so laundry day becomes "tent city" as wet sheets and towels are draped on furniture in their apartment. They don't have money to pick up prepared food for meals, so it is always "cooking from scratch," which takes much longer. Sometimes they run out of money for food before the next payday. Their children don't have money for extracurricular activities at school unless they can earn the money through odd jobs. All four of her children worked on farms last summer so there would be more food for the family. Because it is a new experience for this family to live in poverty, Ann is keenly aware of how much work it takes just to get by.

As I reflected on her experiences and the judgments heaped on struggling families, I tried to understand why people want to think of those in poverty as lazy. I believe they do it as a form of self-protection. They know that they themselves are not lazy; so, if the people in poverty are lazy, then they themselves will never be poor because they are willing to work hard. It is self-protection—and self-delusion—that lead to this judgment. Ann demonstrates that they are wrong. Laziness is not possible for people who know in their bones the daily struggles of poverty.

So, if we are to address the bondage of income and wealth disparities in our nation, what would emancipation look like? We have heard of the Occupy Movement, and "the 99% versus the 1%." We have heard of Mitt Romney's statement that 47% of the nation are takers. We have heard much about "them and us," yet my faith experience in the contemplative journey has led me to know that we are all connected. There is no division between us and them. For real emancipation to occur, we must bridge the gaps that divide us.

Emancipation means freedom from the harsh judgments that bind all of us.

My recent spiritual work is to radically accept everyone—even those whom I personally find worthy of being "voted off the island." I have come to learn that, if I am at odds with God in an adversary, I am at odds with God in me. That means that I need to open my heart to the CEO and politicians as well as to Ann and Robin. I am called to have a heart of compassion for those who judge struggling families as lazy, as well as to care for those who live every day in poverty.

Radical acceptance calls me to care for the 100%. For me, this means hearing the stories of people whom I would rather leave out of my circle of care. Hearing the stories of politicians who want to eliminate the social safety net is key to understanding them and their politics. Hearing the stories of CEOs is essential to changing our toxic economy. In short, hearing the stories of people I might not want to care about is essential to moving forward toward freedom for the common good.

Touching the real pain of all is at the heart of the movement toward emancipation. But it can't stop there. There is a second component to this journey toward freedom: fight! Too often we think of fighting as "fighting against." I have learned that when you "fight against" someone or some policy, that person or policy may actually be reinforced. Rather, in this spiritual journey toward emancipation, we are called to fight *for* a vision that can be shared. We fight *for* a world that is inclusive of all creation. We fight *for* an economy of inclusion. This is why Dr. King's "I Have a Dream" speech was so seminal: He articulated a hunger that transcended the polarization of the time and described a new Promised Land.

It is my experience that we realize emancipation when we combine radical acceptance with fighting for a vision. Embracing all with care and fighting for an economy that benefits the 100% will liberate us from the shackles of polarization and division. In my experience, these events become like a communal fire. There is a flaming-up of community dedicated to the good of all. It is fire in the warmth of the care we share with each other and in the commitment to make a difference. It is a fire that frees us from fear, judgment, and isolation, and opens us to the freedom of an abundant universe.

Then we become quite like the burning bush in Exodus. When the God of radical acceptance and fight flames up in our lives, God speaks through us to say: "I have indeed seen the misery of my people. I have heard them crying for help on account of their taskmasters. Yes, I am well aware of their sufferings. And I have come" (Ex 3:7-8a).

Letting God flame up in our lives, following the liberating call of loving acceptance and fighting for a vision, has consequences. The first time I went to see Congressman Paul Ryan, after spending two weeks on a bus challenging his budget proposal in 2012, I took my Bible with me. I got to his office early and was nervously standing in the hall. I opened the Scripture to the Exodus story for sustenance and, for the first time, read further. Yikes! As I turned the page, I read, "So now I'm sending you to Pharaoh." Moses immediately asks, "Who am I to go to Pharaoh?" "I shall be with you" is the response (Ex 3:10-12).

I completely agree with Moses! Who am I (or any of us) to go to Pharaoh? The fact is that the contemplative journey calls us beyond ourselves—to have a heart for the whole. It is this embrace of all that gives birth to action for the 100%. My experience is that, when I open myself to the deeper story, it is not an academic exercise; rather, it has life-changing consequences. Radical acceptance and fighting for a vision demand engagement in the process that leads to emancipation.

So too, in our time of being shackled by income and wealth disparity, we are called to let God flame up in our lives. Emancipation happens when our contemplative journey takes us beyond ourselves into care for all and fighting for a vision that benefits the 100%. This is not some privatized practice; instead, at the heart, it is the obligation to act on what we know. I am continuously challenged to go to Pharaoh. I am repeatedly comforted that I am not left orphaned.

The emancipation proclamation of our day is that together we must end the shackles of income and wealth disparity in our nation and around the world. This one body of creation is in a single great struggle. Through a radical acceptance of all in love and fighting for a vision, we can be the fire that warms our world and heals our divisions.

Sink into your being. Listen deeply to where you are called to act. Join me in the quest for emancipation from an economy of exclusion. Join me in making different choices for our nation and advocating for justice for the 100%. This is the emancipation for which we long.

The contemplative life is faith in action. We hold the keys to the shackles...listen deeply and act! •

Schooling the Heart

By Timothy P. Shriver

Education is the lure of the transcendent.
—Dwayne Heubner

THE MOST IMPORTANT lessons in life are taught by the least-likely teachers. For instance, I was led to believe that I would learn about equality by studying the work of people like Thomas Jefferson and John Locke. As it turned out, I never understood equality until I encountered Loretta Claiborne, a woman with an intellectual disability, who never wrote a book but who managed to show me that she (and I) counted just as much as everyone else—that we were really all equal. I thought I'd learn about grit and perseverance if I studied Nobel laureates and CEOs, but it was Donal Page, an Irish man who can neither walk nor talk, who showed me what determination truly is. He performed one of the greatest athletic feats I've ever seen: He lifted a bean bag and moved it eighteen inches. The big lessons don't usually come from textbooks; they come from the heart.

We live in a culture that is missing out on those big lessons. We ask schools to test children relentlessly on math and reading—

important topics, to be sure. But we are befuddled when asked to evaluate whether our children are happy or anxious, inspired or disengaged, loved or loners, believers or despairing.

For decades, scholars of both child development and education have focused on understanding attachment, cognition, retention, and technology. These experts have worked to figure out how society should construct educational settings so that children are supported and challenged. They've created hundreds of programs designed to get more "time on task," yet a question they have rarely asked or studied is, "How might we raise children to be free?" Another version of the same question is, "How can we stop destroying the freedom with which children are born?"

The time to ask—and answer—these critically important questions is now. In the past, we've never shied away from teaching the ideals of political freedom and the importance of every individual's right to be *free from* the state and the government. We've been less comfortable, however, with teaching the ideals of transcendent freedom and the importance of every individual's desire to be *free to be* his or her true and best self, and to give that self to goodness, beauty, wisdom, and love. Without realizing it, we've overlooked the universal wellspring of human motivation: the "lure of the transcendent," the longing to be free in an existential or transcendent way—free to be our true selves; free to seek the things that matter most.

I'd like to see schools of the future be places where the "lure of the transcendent" is an integral part of day-to-day teaching and learning—places where people such as Donal and Loretta are teachers in that pursuit. For this vision to become a reality, we need first to define the lure of "transcendence" not as one particular religion's version of seeking God but instead, as the universal longing of the human spirit to seek what is beyond our reach. We must come to understand that transcendence includes the desire to seek what is true and real, beautiful and good, lasting and worthwhile; to live in peace and unity; to love others and creation. Transcendence centers on our capacity for non-dual consciousness and the tantalizing possibility of experiencing that consciousness, at least partially, in the world as we know it now. Donal and Loretta are experts at cracking open our hearts to a transcendent consciousness.

They needn't be alone. Teachers must be trained to encourage children to seek transcendence and non-dual consciousness, since the hunger for transcendence is the source of all human motivation. The longing for transcendence is the wellspring of all our questioning, and of our desire to learn. When teachers tap into that hunger in each child, they tap into the child's most powerful engine of learning. When they fail to tap into a child's hunger for things that matter, learning is reduced to little more than performing a task for the satisfaction of others.

What would it look like to create a practice of educating our children in a way that engages each child in seeking transcendence and learning to be his or her true self?

Happily, we are well on our way. For the last three decades, a growing number of researchers and educators have been developing a new approach, called "Social and Emotional Learning" (SEL), designed to engage the whole child in education. Their goal is to help each child understand his or her emotional and social life and, in so doing, to allow teachers and students to tap into their most powerful feelings, longings, and goals. SEL practices are rooted in psychology and education and they integrate insights from disciplines as diverse as mindfulness, medicine, service learning, and character development. The best evidence-based SEL programs promote relationships of trust and interdependence in classrooms and school cultures.

A framework from the Collaborative for Academic, Social, and Emotional Learning (CASEL[1]) suggests that the core components of promoting the social and emotional development of children in schools fall into five categories:

- **Self-awareness**: The ability to accurately recognize one's emotions and thoughts and their influence on behavior. This includes accurately assessing one's strengths and limitations and possessing a well-grounded sense of confidence and optimism.

- **Self-management**: The ability to regulate one's emotions, thoughts, and behaviors effectively in different situations. This includes managing stress, controlling impulses, motivating oneself, and setting and working toward achieving personal and academic goals.

- **Social awareness**: The ability to take the perspective of and empathize with others from diverse backgrounds and cultures, to understand social and ethical norms for behavior, and to recognize family, school, and community resources and supports.

- **Relationship skills**: The ability to establish and maintain healthy and rewarding relationships with diverse individuals and groups. This includes communicating clearly, listening actively, cooperating, resisting inappropriate social pressure, negotiating conflict constructively, and seeking and offering help when needed.

- **Responsible decision-making**: The ability to make constructive and respectful choices about personal behavior and social interactions based on consideration of ethical standards, safety concerns, social norms, the realistic evaluation of consequences of various actions, and the well-being of self and others.

At first glance, this framework may appear to lack depth. Skills such as "managing stress" or "resisting inappropriate social pressure" might seem to be shallow ways of inviting the "lure of the transcendent" into the classroom, but a closer look is worthwhile.

Self-awareness," for example, is often taught by helping children explore their feelings in depth through inviting them to journal about or name difficult emotions. Teachers invite children to explore their inner lives openly, honestly, and without shame. Similarly, self-management may sound mechanical, yet often includes teaching children how to find silence, calm, and a sense of inner spaciousness. These lessons are taught through quiet breathing, mindfulness meditation, nature walking, and artistic expression. Responsible decision-making often includes teaching children how to serve others with openness and solidarity.

In traditional classrooms, where math or literature may be the subjects, these kinds of lessons do far more than introduce new skills or standards for learning; they invite both teacher and student to bring all aspects of themselves into the classroom, including their biggest dreams, their wildest hopes, their darkest fears, their most generous selves. And in many cases, SEL classroom lessons are complemented by school wide activities that celebrate self-expression, help-seeking, nonviolent mediation, and community service—all as ways of building upon each child's chances of growing and developing in healthy and positive ways. When children and adults find themselves fully engaged

How can we stop destroying the freedom with which children are born?

and supported in these endeavors, deep learning can take place in ways that are far more satisfying, successful, and enduring.

However, this framework is far from complete; significant energy must be applied to make this type of learning into a standard of education. In each of the SEL categories, for example, there are scholars and educators who are developing new learning experiences that get closer to teaching the idea of freedom—from fear, anxiety, anger, and all the things that make learning difficult. The SEL framework is dynamic and open to revision and improvement, so the time is right for the thousands of us who seek non-duality and a unified field of consciousness to offer further insights. What are the lessons we should add to the SEL framework to make it more effective at teaching goodness and love? What might it look like to have a curriculum that would allow every school to become a "school of the heart"?

Needless to say, it won't be easy, but nothing important ever is. I doubt there is any challenge more important for families, communities, and countries than learning how to motivate and inspire our young people. We are in the midst of a great crisis of confidence in our institutions, our culture, and our leaders, and we are seeking new paradigms that offer new ways for young people to find fulfillment and meaning. No one needs a sense of purpose and belonging more than our children do.

While the challenge is great, we *can* meet it. I'm reminded of hearing the great Archbishop Desmond Tutu speak at a gathering years ago. Someone asked him where he got his confidence in the goodness of God, when there is so much evil and despair in the world. His answer moved me to confidence. I don't recall his exact words, but I can paraphrase from memory: "We always think of evil as being more powerful than good, but it is not more powerful! Good is more powerful than evil! Yes, good is more powerful than evil. But we must acknowledge one thing: evil tends to be better organized. If we intend good things for the world and for each other, we too must be organized."

It is time for us to teach these great lessons to children. I can just imagine Loretta Claiborne's classes on self-respect and equality, taught with the words of a woman who has "fallen upward" to sharpen her heart's vision of human beauty. So too, I can imagine Donal Page's class on grit, taught without words, but instead with his relentless and fearless effort to complete what some might consider a simple task. In these and other lessons, children will learn the gifts of courage, wisdom, and gratitude that come from within.

When we finally open our schools to the lessons of the heart, we will at last give our children the chance to pursue what matters most: their deepest hungers and thirsts, their ways of becoming fully alive. When we do that, they will learn not only the subjects of math, science, social studies, and language, but also the subject of life. •

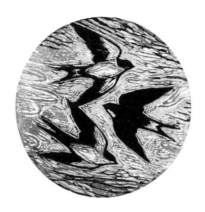

Recipe Cards, Remembrance, and Emancipation

By Paul Fromberg

RECIPE CARDS INVITE an anamnetic relationship between the original author and the cook in the kitchen. In order to use these cards, one must transcend a merely scientific attempt at cookery and enter into a place of deep remembrance and creativity. The Eucharist and the meals promised by my grandmother's recipe cards are each incomplete; they need the participation of hungry, creative people who will make real the promise that they contain. Each recipient of the Sacrament must appropriate the grace of the meal in his or her own lived experience and create from that experience something new: an improvisation in life of the grace of God.

My grandmother was a self-trained artist. At the beginning of the day, wearing a dressing gown, her hair in curlers, she would dispatch her children to school and her husband to the office. She would remain this way for most of the day, not fulfilling the role of "housewife," but making art. She would paint and sculpt, work that set her heart and mind free from domestic drudgery. Only at the end of the day, as her children came home from school, would she dress, quickly straighten the house, and prepare the evening meal. She would greet my grandfather at the door, appearing to have spent the day in typical domestic tasks which she literally accomplished in the final moments before his arrival. Her art mattered more than her housework; it was emancipatory work for her.

Cooking was a part of her art. My grandmother was a splendid cook. She could bake, fry, stew, roast, preserve, pickle, can, and jar just about anything. She cooked almost every day of her life, at least until she was debilitated by the cancer that eventually caused her death. The great sadness for her at the end of her life was that food lost its taste. She could no longer enjoy the flavor of fried catfish or carrot cake, of chicken and dumplings or buttermilk pie. When she died, her estate was divided among her children, grandchildren, and great-grandchildren. On her kitchen wall hung a cross-stitch panel that defined her cooking style: "I Love to Cook Without a Book." Although my sister received this family artifact in the division of my grandmother's estate, I received something of equal value: her collection of recipe cards and their storage box, on which she painted hearts, fruit, vegetables, and even a set of salt and pepper shakers.

The recipes are handwritten on scraps of paper: old envelopes, grocery-store receipts, and the like. Hardly any of the instructions are complete; instead, they are notes to an accomplished artist, each one requiring improvisation as well as memory. Each one invites newness and creativity. Womanist and Feminist scholars teach us that domestic, cultural objects are valuable for transmitting history. Such objects evoke a memory of creative action, liberation, and beauty. For women of my grandmother's generation, this truth is essential. These women had less access to the instruments of history and memory, so the objects that they created are crucial in transmitting their stories.

My grandmother was the matriarch of my family. She inspired children and grandchildren by her words as well as her work. When I was young, I would visit her home in the country and spend countless hours in a process of creative exploration, painting, making, and puttering in her studio, which she called "The Art House." This was emancipatory

When we gather for the Eucharist today, it is as a people who are beginning to learn what it means to be free.

time for me: moments in which my heart and mind were set free. It was not only the freedom of sharing wisdom with a creative soul, not only the eating of delicious food; it was an experience of love. Real love is the birthplace of emancipation.

From time to time, I still cook with my grandmother's recipe cards. When I use them, I am not just participating in an exercise in cooking; I am a part of my grandmother's life and, in a very real sense, extending her love to those whom I love. I share the wisdom of my grandmother's experience and get to participate in her understanding of beauty and creativity. The recipe cards are splattered and smeared by use. At times, a smear is the mark of my grandmother's finger, seemingly trying to wipe the card clean. Like a relic, this patina speaks to the physical presence of my grandmother, transmitted across time and space.

Sharing food works to "re-member" the community. It binds people across time as well as across tables. When I use my grandmother's recipes, remembrance continues. I dine with loved ones on the foods enjoyed by previous generations. We share our own memories of those who are no longer physically present. This is the very definition of anamnesis. The word comes from the Greek *anamnesin,* "remembrance." The idea of anamnesis was first used in relation to the Eucharist by St. Paul, writing in his First Letter to the Corinthians (11:23-25):

> For I received from the Lord what I also handed on to you, that the Lord Jesus on the night when he was betrayed took a loaf of bread, and when he had given thanks, he broke it and said, "This is my body that is for you. Do this in remembrance of me." In the

same way, he took the cup also, after supper, saying, "This cup is the new covenant in my blood. Do this, as often as you drink it, in remembrance of me."

Paul is writing to a community in a pastoral crisis concerning food. During the ritual meal, which we now call the Eucharist, rich people were coming early and eating everything, leaving the poor with nothing. Paul encourages the community to look beyond their personal needs and remember the weaker members of the group. He conflates this remembering of the poor with the memory of Jesus' own gift of life and freedom, given to humanity in his passion, death, and resurrection. In remembering the poor and Jesus' life, Paul says that the community becomes the Body of Christ. As the Body of Christ, the community lives out its identity as the real presence of Jesus in the world. As community members act for the sake of freedom in the world, Jesus is alive and active with and in them.

The sense of remembrance that Paul has in mind is active. It is much more than a cognitive exercise of pulling together facts about a past event; it is an embodied experience that brings the event being remembered into the present. It is about the way that God has emancipated people from their slavery, setting them free in a world of love, peace, justice, and beauty. Paul's teaching is contiguous with the annual celebration of the Passover. In the Passover meal, people are instructed to claim, through remembrance, God's liberation of their ancestors from slavery into freedom. Again, this is not only a cognitive exercise; it is standing with the ancestors in their deliverance from slavery into freedom. It remembers emancipation.

When we gather for the Eucharist today, it is as a people who are beginning to learn what it means to be free. We hear the stories of redemption in the Hebrew Scriptures, the signs and wonders of the Kingdom wrought by Jesus in the Gospels, and the non-compliance of the early church in the narrative of empire in the Epistles, we become aware of an historical counter-narrative with eschatological and emancipatory overtones. The repetition of sacred story as part of the Eucharist reinforces a new narrative in the imagination of worshippers.

Anamnesis is not only memory of the past; it projects the community into the future with a sense of hope and trust. The future, which anamnesis also remembers, is about life in God, where all people join in celebrating their emancipation. The remembrance of the promise binds us to those not yet born who will share our hope of deliverance from slavery to freedom: God's desire for all beings. The prophet Isaiah set this promise in the context of a lavish dinner party (Isaiah 25:6-10a):

> On this mountain the Lord of hosts will make for all peoples
>   a feast of rich food, a feast of well-matured wines,
>   of rich food filled with marrow,
>   of well-matured wines strained clear.
> And he will destroy on this mountain
>   the shroud that is cast over all peoples,
>   the sheet that is spread over all nations;
> he will swallow up death for ever.
> Then the Lord God will wipe away the tears from all faces,
>   and the disgrace of his people he will take away from all the
>   earth,
>   for the Lord has spoken.
> It will be said on that day,
>   Lo, this is our God; we have waited for him,
>   so that he might save us.
>   This is the Lord for whom we have waited;
>   let us be glad and rejoice in his salvation.
> For the hand of the Lord will rest on this mountain.

In this world, the past becomes the present, and the future too. All time is the current moment. In this world, memory is called, not simply from the mind, but from the body. In terms of the Eucharist, it is the action of eating, not the idea of eating, that describes anamnesis. Likewise, it is real emancipation, not just the idea of freedom that is the goal of Eucharistic life. According to anamnesis, our remembering is not just an idea—not just words written on a recipe card—but something that we must do. We take those words, that recipe, and we create something out of it: Eucharist. We remember the event that calls us to act for the sake of emancipation in the world. It is the difference between reading a recipe and enjoying a meal cooked from a recipe. This active remembrance is transformative, acting on us when we may least expect it to do so.

At the end of every day, my grandmother would prepare and knead dough, leave it in the refrigerator overnight to slowly rise, and bake it in the morning for breakfast. I would awaken in my grandmother's house to the smell of bread baking every morning. This process was completely effortless for her, and it was repeated day after day, year after year. It was infused with her love and her life. So, even now, a quarter-century after her death, I can still smell the bread baking and savor its yeasty memory in my imagination. It is a memory that changes me; my mouth waters and my eyes fill with tears, experiences that honor my grandmother. The recipe card transmits the instruction across time and space, such that I need only follow the direction and be returned to childhood.

Bread is at the center of the Eucharist, of course. Along with wine, it is still shared among those who gather at Jesus' table. The story we tell, the story first passed on to us by St. Paul, says that it is in the eating and remembering that we remember the future into which we press, day by day, year after year. In that future, all beings will be emancipated from their slavery to death and live eternally to feast at the banquet prepared by God from the beginning of creation. •

The Freedom of the Greater Heart

By Paula D'Arcy

Our greatest hope for the future rests not in the triumph of any single set of beliefs, but in the acknowledgment of a felt mystery that underlies all our doctrines.
—David Abram, Becoming Animal

THERE IS A LOVE which itself has the power to free the human heart. Many remarkable people live in testament to this love, even though they are held in jail cells and prisons, or suffer the harsh conditions imposed by poverty, adversity, war, and occupation. The truth of this love is that, if we can be uprooted from our daily preoccupations and taken by direct experience into its presence, then a profound transformation is possible. Whoever arrives at this place looks at the world differently. The distinctions on the surface no longer exist. Here it is possible to suspend our certainties and touch something greater: the Spirit within us.

In January 2014, I met the fire of that inner heart. The outer circumstances were the ten days I spent at a retreat center in California with thirty other men and women, brought together by an Israeli-based organization called Together Beyond Words. We were Americans, Mexicans, Israelis, Bedouins, and Palestinians—at least those were the labels we were using, and we kept the story alive by stating and re-stating those identities. We spoke four different languages and had thirty different images of God. We all expressed a longing for freedom, while having little idea what that meant, or might demand. We were about to touch the fire of Spirit, embedded not only deep within our own cells, but in all life. I recorded our journey through those days, and this telling is excerpted from my journal.

The first days of our being together were dominated by a deep pain that seemed to lie coiled inside each of our bodies like a serpent. The facilitator explained that living in a constant atmosphere of trauma and fear builds internal arsenals. With her guidance, unrestrained anger and outrage began to move through the room like a gusting wind. Strong opinions. Arguments. Shouting. Each person's deeply rooted memories and scars. But it was more than that. Deeper, and more affecting, was a shared sense that someone is right and someone else is wrong, along with the sharp fissures that "rightness" creates.

> *My head aches and I want to leave. I want to run far from this conflict and the intimate look at myself that it brings into being. I don't want to see that how I participate in the world is often less than love, and that the environment in which we all live is the result of our sense of entitlement and greed. I don't want to know what freedom demands and what dedication to love and peace may require. Words from the poet Rumi haunt my thoughts: his saying that, in order to live in this world, you have to be truly and completely in love. Well, in this room, we are not in love.*

Freedom is found in discovering the inner identity of the Soul in us that cannot be enslaved.

A beautiful young Jewish woman, delicate, filled with energy and life, begins to cry. "I cannot stand this," *she wails.* "I cannot bear what we're all becoming." *Our instruction has been to get on our feet and move when someone's words touch us. Move and stand behind that person; show support for his or her heart. Most of the room, including me, moves to stand behind her. She is still crying; she cannot stop. I put the palm of my hand on her back. She looks over her shoulder and acknowledges my touch.*

Less than a week earlier, I had been speaking at a conference held in a casino in Reno, Nevada. In the morning, walking through the casino, looking for a breakfast cafe, the vacant stares of those who had been pulling the levers of slot machines all through the night seeped into me. What are we doing? Who are we being? This is what I had begun to ask.

Now, in this room in California, a young Israeli man courageously asks all the Americans in the room—six of us—to come forward. "What are you doing in this country?" *he wants to know. His eyes are steady and striking.* "All the possibility!" *he cries.* "What are you doing? The resources. Your beautiful freedom! You say you are helping the world by shipping weapons. By giving money for arms. By enabling one human being to kill another. This is not real help. It is not real help." *Everyone in the room, including the Americans, moves to stand behind him. Everyone is in tears, the man himself bent double and weeping.*

The feelings being expressed are like a fiery current, a flood tide, with everyone speaking at once, desperate to be heard. And yet, if asked, I myself can't tell by looking who is Arab and who is Jew; who is Bedouin. Someone that morning had spoken to me and said, "Aren't you Jewish?" *It was that crazy: I wouldn't even know where to direct my hatred if I had it.*

I think of how a baby is born without conditioning; it has to be taught. I think of how we cannot stay with our conditioning and heal the pain in our individual lives, much less mend this terribly torn world. I think of how we cannot all keep being right, even in small, silent ways—because they aren't silent. The energy of our rightness permeates the world, even if we never speak it out loud. The energy of our rightness permeates our families, permeates the soil and streams. It becomes the air we breathe and the prison in which we live.

I stand, looking into this young man's shining eyes, and vividly remember when the great darkness of losing my family left me equally brokenhearted—left me terrified and grief-stricken. I remember how justified I felt, in terms of the drunk driver who caused the accident that ended their lives. In those days, I desperately wanted to be released from pain. Not even knowing this man before me, I feel his heart within my own. The voices in the room momentarily fade. I consider that it's not a matter of politics. It's a profound human issue, born of a deep and terrible conditioning in all our hearts, which will only be solved if we arrive at the true, inner heart... and are touched by Love itself. When I met the drunk driver, seven years after the deaths of my husband and daughter—when I glimpsed the power of forgiveness—the touch of that Love turned my life around.

The poet Rilke says that we're grasped by what we cannot grasp, and Thomas Merton writes about being unsure of where he was going—and then the seas opened before his ship. Einstein teaches that no problem is solved using the same consciousness that created it. But these are words we must embody. I reach out my hand to a Mexican woman standing close to me, and to an Arab man on my left. There is nothing in me consciously driving this gesture. Something from deep within is reaching.

Love does not come as theory. It moves in bodies, in nature, in the ground beneath us and the space between. True Love is not emotional. It is a different nature, waiting in us like a secret seed. The illusion is thinking that, by changing a system, an ideology, or our external circumstances, things will change. No; freedom is found in discovering the inner identity of the Soul in us that *cannot* be enslaved. It is realizing that this Love is not a symbol or an ideal; it is a living power.

The days that follow are almost too tender to be held by words. The stories include how exhausted we all felt, once the accusations and emotions ran out of us... once the tears subsided. And then, slowly and imperceptibly, something else began to rise up.

One night, half of us took a midnight walk. Lying on our backs and falling into the gravity of earth, we experienced the coolness of the evening and the gentle wind. We were touched by distant stars. We listened. The next day, rising at 5:00 a.m., some of us watched the moon set over the ocean as the sun rose behind our backs. The moon turned pink before sinking into the sea. In a few hours, patterns of light spread across the grasses and a footbridge. Whales and dolphins appeared in the waters beneath the cliffs, their dance moving deep into our muscles, cradling and transforming the fear. The warm waters of the hot tubs, the light and the dark—it all slowly affected our psyches and our hearts. We danced, hard and fast, all of us mixed in together. People danced with people they'd been conditioned to hate, and felt the pulse of love which is our innate freedom.

Love is not a symbol or an ideal; it is a living power.

    Each day I saw the world anew. We watched clouds and walked slowly through rows of plants in the garden. Everywhere the soul was returning to its depth. It became clear that every conflict we carry is a potential doorway, a gate. Jew. Arab. Christian. Muslim. Druze. The cliffs. The hawk. Everything is a manifestation of divine radiance. Love rushes everywhere, in everyone, in everything. And I understood what it could mean if we met the outer world with our inner world: the very miracle—all life—is awaiting.

    A Mexican woman gave me a small, beautiful stone she'd been carrying. An Arab woman handed me a string of cobalt blue prayer beads. A young Muslim man asked me—for the rest of my life, even if we never met again—if I would pray for his soul.

    The last day. A shawl is spread on the floor in our meeting room. But, before gathering there, we each find a spot in the surrounding woods and sit alone.

    Returning to the room, everyone brings flowers, petals, stones, leaves, and branches to cover the shawl.

You have to be truly and completely in love.

    We sit in a circle around the beauty, and the flowers reflect our own flowering. We are the same small band of humanity who arrived days ago, and yet we are changed. We are gods, opening the world's heart by opening our own. Even if the world around us lives in a dream of war and entitlement, of greed and revenge, in this moment we are not living that dream, and we experience how it feels to touch the greater heart.

    At the end, we stand up and take a few steps backward until we're looking down at the cushions where we have been sitting all week—the cushions of our human identity... our ethnicity... our points of view... our private dreams. My eyes connect with other eyes around the circle. Together we join hands, step across the cushions, and circle the shawl. There are tears, but no hardness. We are the space, we are the opening, we are the ones where the Divine Heart will be born. We are the freedom, waiting to be known.

We've reached into the heart of suffering—our common suffering, entered it, and drawn out the beauty. In that room and within that circle, we touch everything that is.

There is a living love that exceeds our circumstances and our conditioning. That's the truth we all must find. The profound problems of hatred, judgment, and revenge, our jealousies and our violence, will be solved by love, and love alone.

The emancipation of the heart is to know that we were always free. Moving toward love or away from love, we are creating this world. •

Exquisite Risk:
John of the Cross and the Transformational Power of Captivity

By Mirabai Starr

*On a dark night
Inflamed by love-longing—
O, exquisite risk!—
Undetected, I slipped away,
My house, at last, grown still.*[1]

SOMETIMES IT IS in our prisons that we find our freedom. In 1577, when St. John of the Cross was thirty-five years old, he was abducted by his own monastic brothers and incarcerated for nine months in a monastery in Toledo, Spain. It was there, as he languished, that the caterpillar of his old self dissolved and the butterfly of his authentic being grew its wings.

Purgation

Secure in the darkness,
I climbed the secret ladder in disguise—
O, exquisite risk!—
Concealed by the darkness,
*My house, at last, grown still.*²

John was a contemplative and a poet. He was undoubtedly an introvert. But he was also a revolutionary. After six years of his engaged leadership in Teresa of Ávila's efforts to reform the Carmelite order and return it to its roots in desert spirituality, a contingent of Carmelite monks, opposed to the reform, broke into John's dwelling in the middle of the night, dragged him away, and locked him up. His prison cell, a stone room barely large enough for his body, had formerly been a latrine. His single robe rotted from his body in the fetid heat of summer, and in winter he shivered in the rag that remained. Several times a week, the brothers brought him out to be flogged while they enjoyed their midday meal. Otherwise, he sat in the darkness, tracking the stars through the single small window, high up in the wall of his cell.

"Have you heard?" one monk would say to another in a stage whisper outside the locked door of John's cell. "The Reform has been crushed." Or "Teresa is dead." Sometimes they would direct their comments to the prisoner: "You have been forgotten, *Hermano*. Renounce *la Madre* and her wickedness. She doesn't care about you anyway." John did not believe them, and he did not forsake his mentor. At least, he did his best not to believe them.

Doubt began to infiltrate his psyche and, though he clung to the life-raft of faith, it began to disintegrate in his hands and he drifted into despair. Like Jonah in the belly of the fierce fish (an analogy John later evoked when he wrote the commentary to *Dark Night of the Soul*), the imprisoned friar found himself suspended in the void. He was unable to move toward any kind of hopeful future, or backward to the innocent idealism that had led to his being swallowed up in this terrible emptiness.

It was painful enough for him to wonder if God had given up on him, but the true agony descended when he began to find himself giving up on God. At last, he simply ran out of energy and let himself down into the arms of radical unknowingness—which is where the transmutation of the lead of his agony began to unfold into the gold of mystical poetry.

It was poetry that saved him.

Not at first, and not all at once, but little by little. Even as John cried out to a Beloved whose presence he could no longer detect and whose existence made no sense, his longing began to take the shape of words, and the words formed themselves into stanzas. He repeated these poems, again and again, until they were seared into his heart and fixed in his mind.

> Where have you hidden away,
> Beloved, and left me grieving?
> Why would you hurt me, abandon me,
> Fleeing like a deer?
> I rushed after you,
> But my cries only drifted in the empty air.[3]

Like the Bride in the Scripture he loved best—the Song of Songs—John went "tracking the sandal-mark" of his Beloved through the streets and plazas of his ravaged heart and, finding no trace of the One who "wounded his soul and set it on fire," converted his yearning into sublime love-language. It is the fruit of that alchemy that sustained the poet in his imprisonment and has continued to feed the rest of us for five centuries.

Illumination

> *That sweet night: a secret.*
> *Nobody saw me;*
> *I did not see a thing.*
> *No other light, no other guide*
> *Than the one burning in my heart.*
>
> *This light led the way*
> *More clearly than the risen sun*
> *To where he was waiting for me*
> *—the one I knew so intimately—*
> *In a place where no one could find us.*[4]

Finally, a sympathetic guard slipped sheets of parchment, a quill, and ink into John's cell so that he could write down the poems he spent his days reciting. That same Brother probably looked the other way when, one night, after the time it takes for a fertilized egg to ripen into a baby and enter the world, John fashioned a robe from strips of the cloth that covered his pallet, tossed it over the ledge of his high window, and hoisted himself out of hell. He scaled the outer wall, crept across the courtyard, and scrambled over the monastery walls. Legend has it that a black dog was waiting for him—a shadow against the darkness—and led him to one of Teresa's convents in Toledo, where the Sisters swept him into safety and nursed him back to health.

A deep quietude settled on John's soul as he sat in the convent garden in the mornings with the sun on his face, and as he climbed the hill to embrace the night sky he so loved. From this peace arose a wondrous joy, and from that ecstasy, one of the greatest poems in the canon of mystical literature bubbled forth like water from an artesian well: *Songs of the Soul*. From this sensual love poem, at the behest of the Sisters, came one of the most important teachings on the spiritual life ever articulated: the prose commentary known as the *Dark Night of the Soul*.

This is the teaching that saved my life when I was thrown into a prison of my own.

Union

O night, that guided me!
O night, sweeter than sunrise!
O night, that joined lover with Beloved!
Lover transformed in Beloved![5]

Radical loss can be a prison, and grief can feel like a life sentence. Toward the end of 2001, on the very day that my first book came out—a new translation of *Dark Night of the Soul*—my fourteen-year-old daughter, Jenny, was killed in a car accident. I heard the prison gate clang shut as I was plunged into a bondage of the heart so violent that I could not imagine ever being set free to live again among the human family. I could not imagine tasting the essence of a ripe pear, appreciating the beauty of the sunrise after another sleepless winter night, or caring about the fragrance of an infant's hair.

But John of the Cross had taught me just enough to know that my only task was to rest in the Mystery and stop trying to solve the problem of death. My highest calling was to relinquish my attachment to feeling the presence of the Holy One so that the Holy One could do her work in me. Years of contemplative practice had taught me just enough to know not to believe everything I think, or even to expect my practice to save me. Like my spiritual brother John, I closed my eyes and composed silent love poems to a God in whom I no longer believed.

"If only the souls this happens to," says John, referring to the spiritual crisis known as a dark night of the soul, "could just be quiet, setting aside all concern about accomplishing any task—interior or exterior—and quit troubling themselves about accomplishing anything! Soon, within that very stillness and release, they would begin to subtly taste that interior nourishment, a nourishment so delicate that, if they were purposely to try, they could never taste it."[6]

And so I did that. I sat in the center of the conflagration of my heart and watched (with a mixture of self-compassion and mild curiosity) while the flames consumed who I thought I was. Into this wreckage began to seep the "subtle sweetness" of which John spoke. I experienced the breath of my Beloved on my eyelids, the warmth of his hand in my hand. In my unfathomable brokenness, I began to discover my hidden wholeness. My captivity became my emancipation. It was not dramatic; it was subtle, almost imperceptible, but I began to recognize it as a gift of grace, and I said "yes," and I said "thank you."

Annihilation

I lost myself. Forgot myself.
I lay my face against the Beloved's face.
Everything fell away and I left myself behind.
Abandoning my cares
Among the lilies, forgotten.[7]

Not only do we have a tendency to miss the chance to engage our experiences of incarceration as monastic opportunities; the reverse is also true: we resist emancipation. John refers to the Israelites as they crossed the wilderness from captivity in Egypt to freedom in the Promised Land. Every morning, when they awoke, the ground was covered with manna from heaven. Every morsel contained the flavor that each wayfarer most loved. And yet, what did the former slaves spend their days craving? "The meats and onions they ate in Egypt." The food of bondage. We get attached to our inner Pharaohs, as Jewish wisdom teaches us in the Passover liturgy. We settle into the comfortable misery of the familiar prison cells into which we have sentenced ourselves and refuse to embrace the Holy Wildness of spiritual liberation.

My captivity became my emancipation.

The great mystics of all traditions teach us that the spiritual life is not really about consolation; it is about annihilation. It is about allowing the small self, which suffers from the illusion of separation from God, to burn in the flames of transformation so that the True Self may emerge. "In this way," John writes, "God makes the soul die to all that is not inherently of God. When the soul is stripped bare of her old skin, God clothes her afresh. Like the eagle, her youth is revitalized. She is clothed in newness of being."[8]

Our prisons take many forms. Some of us struggle with the very real circumstances of physical incarceration. Many of us suffer from profound losses; not only the death of loved ones, but also serious health diagnoses, or loss of a job, career, or community. We may grapple with chronic mental illness, addiction, or the addictive behaviors of loved ones. Embracing our imprisonment as a chance for a direct encounter with the Sacred is counter-intuitive, but it may be the very blessing we most need for our journey home. Stripped of all sensory and conceptual attachments, freed of our own opinions on the matter, these dark nights of our souls dismantle the obstacles that stand between ourselves and our Beloved. Our only task is to say "yes," no matter how tentatively; to say "thank you," no matter how quietly. •

NOTES

Psalm 5 (a paraphrase)

1 Ernesto Cardenal, "Psalm 5 (a paraphrase)," trans. Robert Marquez, *Twentieth-Century Latin American Poetry: A Bilingual Anthology*, Stephen Tapscott, ed. (Austin: University of Texas Press, 2003), 298–299. Used with permission of Copyright Clearance Center.

The Power of "Yes"

1 Denis Edwards, *Ecology at the Heart of Faith: The Change of Heart that Leads to a New Way of Living on Earth* (Maryknoll, NY: Orbis Books, 2008), 12–13.

2 Philip Clayton, "Neuroscience, the Person, and God: An Emergentist Account," in *Neuroscience and the Person: Scientific Perspectives on Divine Action*, ed. Robert John Russell, Nancey Murphy, Theo C. Meyering, and Michael A. Arbib (Vatican City/Berkeley, CA: Vatican Observatory and Center for Theology and the Natural Sciences, 1999), 211; cf. ibid., *Mind and Emergence: From Quantum to Consciousness* (New York: Oxford University Press, 2004), 38–39.

3 Pierre Teilhard de Chardin, *The Phenomenon of Man*, trans. Bernard Wall (New York: Harper & Row, 1959), 221.

4 Pierre Teilhard de Chardin, *Human Energy*, trans. J. M. Cohen (New York: Harcourt Brace Jovanovich, 1969), 23.

5 Thomas Merton, *New Seeds of Contemplation* (New York: New Directions, 1961), 29.

6 Pope Benedict XVI, "St. Maximus the Confessor," *L'Osservatore Romano* (2 July 2008): 16. http://www.ewtn.com/library/PAPALDOC/b16ChrstChrch75.HTM.

7 Neil Douglas-Klotz, *The Sufi Book of Life* (New York: Penguin Compass, 2006), 181.

Exodus through the Lens of Emancipation

1. Interestingly, the Septuagint titled the second book of the Pentateuch "Exodus." Hebrew tradition titled it "Names."
2. Midrash Shemot Rabbah 1:33.
3. Harriet Beecher Stowe, "A Reply," Atlantic Monthly 11 (January 1863): 120–133, reprinted in Louis P. Mansur, "…the real war will never get in the books": Selections from Writers During the Civil War (New York: Oxford University Press, 1993).
4. James M. McPherson, The Negro's Civil War (New York: Vintage Books, 1965), 228.
5. Leon F. Litwack, Been in the Storm So Long (New York: Alfred A. Knopf, 1979), 64.
6. Frederick Douglass, Narrative of the Life of Frederick Douglass, an American Slave, Written by Himself (Boston: Bedford Books of St. Martin's Press, 1993), 74.
7. Ibid.
8. Linda Brent, Incidents in the Life of a Slave Girl (New York: Harcourt, Brace, Jovanovich, 1973), 63.
9. Carter G. Woodson, The Education of the Negro Prior to 1861 (New York: Arno Press, 1968), 151–178.
10. Litwack, 473.
11. Benjamin A. Quarles, The Negro in the Civil War (New York: Da Capo, 1989), 289–290.

Schooling the Heart

1. Timothy P. Shriver is Chair of CASEL's Board of Directors.

Exquisite Risk: John of the Cross and the Transformational Power of Captivity

1. Mirabai Starr, trans. and intro., Dark Night of the Soul: St. John of the Cross (New York: Riverhead Books, 2003), 23.
2. Ibid., 24.
3. Mirabai Starr, ed., Devotions, Prayers & Living Wisdom: St. John of the Cross (Boulder: Sounds True, 2008), p. 19.
4. Starr, Dark Night of the Soul: St. John of the Cross, 24.
5. Ibid.
6. Ibid., 64.
7. Ibid., 25.
8. Ibid., 141.

…those who hope in the Lord will renew their strength.
They will soar on wings like eagles;
they will run and not grow weary,
they will walk and not be faint.

—Isaiah 40:31

Center for
Action and
Contemplation

A collision of opposites forms the cross of Christ.
One leads downward preferring the truth of the humble.
The other moves leftward against the grain.
But all are wrapped safely inside a hidden harmony:
One world, God's cosmos, a benevolent universe.